THOUGHTS ARE THINGS

BOOKS BY ERNEST HOLMES

Can We Talk to God?

Change Your Thinking, Change Your Life

Creative Ideas

Creative Mind and Success

Effective Prayer

Good for You

How to Change Your Life

How to Use the Science of Mind

Ideas for Living

It Can Happen to You

Questions and Answers on the Science of Mind

The Beverly Hills Lectures

The Magic of the Mind

The Science of Mind

The Science of Mind Approach to Successful Living

The Voice Celestial

This Thing Called Life

This Thing Called You

What Religious Science Teaches

Words That Heal Today

THOUGHTS ARE THINGS

*. . . the things in your life and
the thoughts that are behind them*

Ernest Holmes
and
Willis Kinnear

Health Communications, Inc.
Deerfield Beach, Florida

www.bci-online.com

Library of Congress Cataloging-in-Publication Data

Holmes, Ernest, 1887-1960.
    Thoughts are things : the things in your life and the thoughts that
are behind them / Ernest Holmes and Willis Kinnear.
        p.   cm.
    Includes index.
    ISBN 1-55874-721-4 (pbk.)
    1. New Thought.   I. Kinnear, Willis.   II. Title.
BF639.H6375
299'.93—dc21   99-31859
                                                                                    CIP

ISBN 1-55874-721-4

Publisher: Health Communications, Inc.
          3201 S.W. 15th Street
          Deerfield Beach, FL 33442-8190

R-06-00

Cover design by Larissa Hise
Inside book design by Dawn Grove

CONTENTS

v

Publisher's Note

One of the earliest admonitions to humankind was: "Know thyself." In attempting self-discovery, people became aware that "thoughts are things," and this concept has been expressed in many ways. This idea and Jesus' statement that "as thou hast believed, so be it done unto thee" are still lightly taken. Their full significance and importance in an individual's life is yet to be realized.

This book is an attempt to bring to the attention of the readers many of the varied aspects of their experience of life and the relationship of their thinking to what they experience.

Every thought has its consequence. And every experience has a causative thought behind it. Thoughts *are* things, and all the things in one's life have a thought that precedes them.

The material in this volume can be divided into two parts. *The Challenge*, which appears on the left-hand page illustrates the various problems, challenges and difficulties which everyone faces at one time or another.

The right-hand page is *The Solution*, from the writings of Ernest Holmes, which presents the solutions to them. Dr. Holmes was one of the great metaphysicians and religious philosophers of the twentieth century. His teaching, known as Science of Mind, has had a dramatic influence on contemporary spiritual thought. His technique for effective prayer—spiritual mind treatment—has opened the door to a new way of life for countless thousands of people.

The Challenge pages were written by Willis Kinnear, who was then Editor of *Science of Mind* Magazine and Director of Science of Mind Publishing.

FOREWORD

If you knew how, would you be willing to create happiness, wealth, health and success in your life? If I shared the knowledge about how to do just that, could you accept it? Would you use it?

Well, here's the secret I'm thrilled to share with you: our thinking influences our every experience—thoughts are things. From the simplest things, say grocery lists, to the larger issues of life, love and happiness, what we say, write, believe, think ... must become the circumstances of our living.

That's why I love this book by Dr. Ernest Holmes; it's so important to the spiritual freedom of every man, woman and child. Without preaching, it teaches us how to transform the personal challenges of fear, anger, jealousy and uncertainty into courage, acceptance, compassion and confidence. This book will lead you from chaos to harmony.

Ernest Holmes was one of the most important spiritual philosophers of this century. He melded the wisdom of the ages into a modern, practical, pragmatic approach to living life to the fullest. No bowing or scraping required here. Thinking—

our everyday practice—is the key to a full, rich, fulfilling, lavish life.

I invite you to take this book home with you, read it again and again, practice its valuable insights. You will be changed by your transformed thinking. Go ahead! You deserve it!

Rev. Kathianne Lewis

[EDITORS' NOTE: *Rev. Kathianne Lewis is Minister of the Center for Spiritual Living, a dynamic church for spiritual seekers in Seattle, Washington.*]

Thoughts are things, so we find that different kinds of thoughts become different kinds of things.

Thought is always creative; it must always create after its own type. It must always give form to something, and the something to which it gives form is not a thing of itself, because the thought that creates the form is a product of the thinker. The thinker comes first, then the thought, and then the form.

—ERNEST HOLMES

I

The World Around You

You are immersed in the immense activity of living. There is a continual challenge of securing from the world around you the things that make life worthwhile, and the incessant demands that your environment makes upon you.

This constant interplay can never be avoided, for it is the very essence of being alive. Whether it is a pleasurable experience or one of continual conflict is the ever-present decision constantly facing you.

Some individuals, in spite of the pressures and vicissitudes of the world about them, are able to master them and literally become masters of their own lives. Others seem to let life overwhelm them, seem to be as lost and helpless as a small rudderless craft in a storm-swept sea. The difference can be traced to a way of thinking.

Are you slave or master? Do you let external situations control you? Or do you control them? Through right well-directed patterns of thought, life can become a joyous daily challenge.

How Do You Think About Yourself?

Have you ever become the least bit concerned or interested in what you think about yourself? If not, it might be to your advantage to give your thinking a good going-over.

In a British medical journal, *The Practitioner,* an article specifically pointed out that doctors should be very careful about what they think about their patients, for there is a strong indication that in some way patients appear to react according to the doctor's thoughts about them. If the doctor thinks that the patients will not get better, this seems to be transferred to the patients' attitude, and they do not get better.

As for the relationship of this idea to our thinking, it cannot be overemphasized that if what another thinks about us has an effect on what we experience, then how much greater effect our own thought has on our experience! We live according to the patterns of thought that we maintain. If we find that our ideas are constantly dwelling on ill-health, failure and bad relationships, is it any wonder that we never seem to be able to get away from such experiences?

There is little we can do about what others think about us, but we can do a lot about what we think about ourselves. Can we possibly afford to think of ourselves other than in a manner that maintains a mental picture of the best possible experiences we could desire? We encounter enough difficulties in everyday living without going to the trouble of creating additional ones through the negative nature of our thought. If we want to be influential people we must start influencing ourselves. But be sure the influencing is in the right direction.

∞

Identity

Your knowledge that the great I Am is ever available gives you an increasing capacity to draw upon It, and to become inwardly aware of the presence of Spirit within you. Through the quiet contemplation of the omniaction of Spirit, learn to look quietly and calmly upon every false condition, seeing through it to the invisible side of Reality which molds conditions and re-creates all of your affairs closer to a Divine pattern.

With a penetrating spiritual vision you can dissipate the obstruction, remove the obstacle, dissolve the wrong condition.

SAY: I now claim health instead of sickness, wealth instead of poverty, happiness instead of misery.

In such degree as I gain mastery over the sense of negation, whether it be pain or poverty, I am proving the Law of Mind in action.

Every thought of fear or limitation is removed from my consciousness.

I know that my word transmutes every energy into constructive action, producing health, harmony, happiness and success.

I know there is something at the center of my being which is absolutely certain of itself.

It has complete assurance and it gives me complete assurance that all is well.

I maintain my position as a Divine Being, here and now.

Science, *Plus*

The wonderful strides science has made in recent years have opened up for us many new worlds of knowledge. Many things that once seemed impossible are now commonplace. New and better ways of doing things have become everyday headlines. We no longer seem surprised by a new discovery, for we have come to expect that science can always do what it wants to do. Regardless of what our problem may be we feel that science has the answer for it.

Science does have a lot of answers, and more will be forthcoming. We are entirely justified in looking to science for help in many ways, but can we count on it to supply all the answers we may need?

Gunnar Gunderson, M.D., past president of the American Medical Association, has made the remarkable statement that we cannot live by science alone, and that cold, crisp scientific methods satisfy neither the doctor nor the patient. Something else is needed. The doctor says that there needs to be warmth, sympathy, understanding and faith.

". . . Man shall not live by bread alone. . . ." It takes more than food to make us happy, and more than a pill to make us healthy. This "more" is love and faith, and neither of these can science in any way supply. We alone are able to provide the experience of love, and this we can do only as we learn to rid our emotions of all fear, resentment, hate and anger. We need to have faith that Life is expressing Itself in and through us in all Its perfection. Without the feeling of love, and without the faith and conviction that Life in us is unobstructed, all the healing techniques of science are of little avail.

∞

Dominion

You know that there is a God-Power at the center of everyone's being, a Power that knows neither lack, limitation nor fear, sickness, disquiet nor imperfection. But because you are an individual you can build a wall of negative thoughts between yourself and this perfection. The wall which keeps you from your greater good is built of mental blocks, cemented together by fear and unbelief, mixed in the mortar of negative experience. It is not necessary that impoverishment and pain must accompany you in your experience through life.

SAY: I know that there is a Presence, a Power and a Law within me, irresistibly drawing everything into my experience which makes life worthwhile.

I know that friendship, love and riches, health, harmony and happiness are mine.

I know that nothing but good can go out from me, therefore the good that I receive is but the completion of a circle—the fulfillment of my desire for all.

I refuse to judge according to appearances, either mental or physical, no matter what the thought says, or what the appearance seems to be.

There is always a higher Power.

Upon this Power I rely with absolute confidence that It will never fail me.

I repudiate all evil, cast out every fear that accompanied it and continuously exercise the dominion which rightfully belongs to me.

Enjoy Living

It is a well-known fact that a great many people indulge in sickness in order to avoid active participation in living. For instance, there are those who develop all the symptoms of heart disease when they are unable to achieve their objectives, but careful examination fails to reveal the actual condition itself. This is an aspect of the well-known escape mechanism which we all use from time to time to keep from doing those things which we do not want to do.

In situations of this kind it is wise to keep in mind the basic nature of Life Itself. To begin with, Life is an active creative process; the minute Its activity is diminished a sort of stagnation sets in and vitality is greatly reduced. Our ability to think is an activity of Life within us. So it follows that when thought ceases to be a constructively creative endeavor there will also be a reduced experience of living.

We should always enter into the matter of living to a greater degree, never to a lesser degree. If we find ourselves withdrawing from things that should be done we are only withdrawing from a fuller experience of the vitality of Life within us. This of course does not mean that we must continually grit our teeth and plow into our unpleasant tasks. Rather we should approach such tasks with a different attitude so that they would not be unpleasant.

As long as we permit ourselves to consider any aspect of living a distasteful activity, and desire to withdraw from it, we are only depriving ourselves of a fuller enjoyment of the things we do desire to experience.

∞

Life

It is only as you live affirmatively that you can be happy. Knowing that there is but one Spirit in which we all live, move and have our being, you are to feel this Spirit not only in your consciousness but in your affairs. You are united with all. You are one with the eternal Light Itself. The Presence of Spirit within you blesses everyone you meet, tends to heal everything you touch, brings gladness into the life of everyone you contact. Therefore you are a blessing to yourself, to humankind and to the day in which you live.

SAY: Today I uncover the perfection within me. In its fullness I reveal the indwelling Kingdom. I look out upon the world of my affairs, knowing that the Spirit within me makes my way both correct and easy.

I know there is nothing in me that could possibly obstruct or withhold the Divine circuit of Life and Love, which God is.

My word dissolves every negative thought or impulse that could throw a shadow over my perfection.

Wisdom shines through my thoughts and actions.

Life harmonizes my body so that it is revitalized and manifests perfection in every cell, organ and function.

Love harmonizes my mind so that joy sings in my heart.

I am in complete unity with Good.

Free Insurance

Today it is possible to buy insurance to cover almost every situation so as to be remunerated for any possible loss. In fact, our desire to protect ourselves from loss has resulted in insurance being one of the really big businesses today.

In many instances the premiums we pay for such protection are a drain on our pocketbooks but we feel that it is money well spent. When losses do occur and an insurance policy does pay off, there is a great feeling of satisfaction that we have protected ourselves in this manner. However, insurance policies are of no value unless disaster hits us. Wouldn't it be wonderful if we were able to provide ourselves with insurance which would protect us against the possibility of disaster occurring?

To a large extent such insurance is available to us. And the premium is not prohibitive in price. In fact, no money is involved at all. It is free as far as money is concerned, but not free in another way. We have to take the time and make the effort to pay for it by keeping a careful guard over our thoughts and emotions.

We can provide ourselves with free insurance which has a fine guarantee of good health. But we need to wake up to the fact that good health is our natural state, and also stop continually inviting sickness with undue worries, concerns and anxieties. The same thing applies also to our relationships and affairs. We can insure their continued good state by not emotionally and mentally nurturing their opposites.

It is never too late to sell yourself some good free insurance.

∞

Security

Do not be like Job, who exclaimed: ". . . the thing which I greatly feared is come upon me. . . ." Instead, release your fears and know that the Mind of God guides you in everything you do and makes the path ahead of you one of joy, happiness and security. Your life is always in the hands of God, and if you permit you will be led in ways that protect you and safely carry you through every experience.

SAY: I know that Divine Intelligence now helps me to control my thinking and causes me to expect only good things to come into my experience.

As I now accept Its guidance It flows through me and out into everything I do and into every situation.

I know that today and every day the Power of the Living Spirit makes perfect the way before me.

Divine Intelligence is always acting upon my mind, telling me what best to do, counseling me wisely and guiding me gently but surely into pathways of prosperity, happiness and physical health.

I am ever protected by the Love of God; I am secure in the hands of God.

Every sense of anxiety and insecurity is now dissolved and fades away.

Only good comes to me and goes out from me.

This is what I expect.

This is what I accept as my experience.

Mental Ability

Most of us appear to have a fair degree of mental ability. But a lot of people have the strange notion that it diminishes with the years. In a research project conducted by the Office of Naval Research, it was ascertained that in all probability this capacity will be much greater at fifty than it was at twenty, and further, that intellectual capacities appear to grow with maturity. Of course this is great news for all of us over the age of twenty. We are not falling apart mentally after all—unless we *let* ourselves do so.

This is a pleasant thought to keep tucked away in an accessible part of our memory. Apparently the only thing that can hinder our ability to think is to think that we are losing the ability. However, the catch in this whole thing is the assumption that to begin with we developed any mental ability at all. Did the wheels ever start going around? Have the billions of nerve cells in the brain ever been used to any great degree? We all like to think that we think, but are our thoughts like a phonograph record which keeps repeating itself with monotonous regularity? Do we only know one tune and keep playing it over and over?

In some respects we all have this problem. But we do have the capacity to deal with new ideas, to expand our horizon of knowledge. And now is always the time to start to use this faculty. It is like developing stronger muscles; the more we use them, the more we will be able to use them. And it seems that as time goes on the more we think, the more we will be able to think.

So start thinking and keep right on thinking in bigger and better ways all the rest of your days.

∞

Inspiration

The disciple John tells us that Jesus said, "God is a Spirit: and they that worship him must worship him in spirit and in truth." Wonderful indeed is the conception of the union of all life, which Jesus proclaimed in the ecstasy of his illumination: "I and my Father are one." All cause and all effect proceed from the invisible Spirit. You are one with this Spirit and cannot be separated from It. Your word has power because your word is the action of God through your thought.

SAY: I now clarify my vision and purify my thought so that it becomes a mirror reflecting inspiration direct from the secret place of the Most High at the center of my own being.

I do this by quiet contemplation, not through strenuous effort but by learning to fast to all negation and to feast upon the affirmations of spiritual realization.

I know that I need never break before the onslaught of any confusion that exists around me.

Today I walk in the light of God's Love.

I am guided and my guidance is multiplied.

There is an inspiration within me which governs every act, every thought, in certainty, with conviction and in peace.

I know that the key that unlocks the treasure-house, the key to the kingdom of God, is in my spiritual hand, and I enter in and experience it today.

This is the kingdom of God's creation.

Protect Yourself

We have many things to defend ourselves against in the matter of living, but we are now told that one of the most important is the infectious nature of the ideas and emotions of others. An editorial in the *Journal of the American Medical Association* stated that mental health and mental illness are just as infectious as a smile or the measles. The implications of this idea for all of us cannot be overlooked.

Of course we are using the term "infected" in two different ways. We may allow ourselves to catch another's happiness or sadness, confidence or fears, stability or instability. If we permit ourselves to become infected with another's fears, this is what we in turn are able to pass on to others. It is staggering to think of what proportions a chain reaction of this kind could grow into. Then there is the hopeful idea that good factors are equally infectious and could be passed on the same way.

Regardless of how contagious another person's negative way of thinking may be, we all have a certain resistance factor within us. To a large degree we are able to determine whether we will permit ourselves to become "infected." We need to develop our mental and emotional stability to the point where we do not allow ourselves to catch unwanted mental attitudes of others which in turn throw our body completely out of balance and leave us wide open for serious physical problems. Conversely, the good things we might catch from another could promote our health and well-being.

From your personal point of view, the thing to remember is that you alone determine what ideas you are going to be susceptible to, and to what degree you will absorb them. Don't get infected by the wrong kind!

∞

Constructive Ideas

It is impossible for you to experience the full joy of living while you identify yourself with anything less than that. The images of your thought attract to you, and you are attracted to people, circumstances and situations which are like them. Once you fully realize this you will understand that to change undesirable conditions, or to protect yourself from them, you must of necessity change the basic pattern of your thought.

This requires that you must constantly be on guard as to what you allow to enter your mind, or arise from negative memories of the past. When such thoughts are in any way contrary to your greatest good they must be immediately discarded and replaced with their opposites, those ideas affirming only your welfare in every respect.

SAY: I know that I am a Son or Daughter of the Most High.

I am one with the Intelligence and Perfection that is back of everything.

As it is the nature of thought to externalize itself, bringing about conditions which exactly correspond to the thought, I affirm that my thoughts are Divinely guided.

I entertain only constructive ideas; all others I willingly discard.

I am aware that there is a Principle of Perfection at the center of my being, an invisible Presence that forever externalizes Itself for me and through me in every avenue of my life, today and every day.

Good Behavior

We all expect good behavior on the part of others and continually emphasize its importance in our children. And for the most part we feel that we behave pretty well ourselves. But do we? Or are we just kidding ourselves? Outwardly we may appear to behave well but the behavior that counts the most can't be seen. Just how well disciplined is our thinking? It's probably far more unruly than we realize!

Dwight L. Wilbur, M.D., of the American College of Physicians, has stated that one-third to two-thirds of the people who visit a doctor's office have no recognizable organic illness. He does not mean by this that their condition is imaginary, but rather that it is a functional disturbance brought on by their way of thinking.

Time and again we find ourselves confronted with the question: What are we doing to ourselves by the way we permit ourselves to think? And the answer more often than not is: More harm than good. Not only do we upset our body by the way we think, but we also seem to be able to adversely affect every situation in which we find ourselves. We spend endless amounts of time complaining about our problems of one kind or another, but seldom go to the trouble to seek out the thoughts that have caused them. Until we step in and discipline our thinking, the same old monotonous ideas will keep repeating themselves, and our problems will not clear up.

At any time, we can start educating our thinking in the fundamentals of good behavior. It is a simple process of thinking about what we want rather than what we don't want. Our experiences in living are the results of ideas we entertain in mind, so we all need to make our thoughts behave properly.

∞

Guidance

Good is at the root of everything, regardless of its seeming absence. But this good must be recognized. Since there is but one Spirit and this Spirit is in you and in everything, then everywhere you go you will meet this Spirit. You meet this Spirit in people, in places and in things. This one Spirit, which manifests Itself in and through all, including yourself, automatically adjusts parts to the whole.

Therefore, you may accept with positive certainty that the Spirit within you does go before you and prepares your way. Your faith is placed in *something* positive, certain as the laws of life, exact as the principles of mathematics. It is the vital, living Force that supports your every thought and deed when they are in harmony with It.

SAY: I know that the Spirit within me goes before me, making perfect, plain, straight, easy and happy the pathway of my experience.

There is nothing in me that can obstruct the Divine circuits of Life, of Wholeness and Perfection.

My affirmative word dissolves every negative thought or impulse that would throw a shadow of imperfection across the threshold of my experience.

I identify myself only with the Living Spirit—with all the Power, all the Presence and all the Life there is.

I lift my cup of acceptance, knowing that the Divine outpouring will fill it to the brim.

Resources

For living to be a joyous experience it now appears that the individual must always be engaged in some sort of creative activity. We can keep busy with many things that consume time and occupy our thoughts, but in the long run there is lacking that sense of satisfaction which comes only as a result of having accomplished something creative and worthwhile.

In this connection, Dr. Eleanor Crissey of Cornell University advances the idea that individuals who are approaching the time of retirement should have developed inner as well as outer resources to draw upon. She feels that creative activity is very vital and must be entered into just for the sheer joy of doing it.

From one point of view the desire and need to be creative is not acquired but is natural to all of us. If we don't recognize it, or do nothing about it, there seems to be a void in our lives. Creativity appears to be a necessity for all people. A child likes to make things, even if it is only mud pies. Young, middle-aged and elderly people must find ways, means and channels through which they can constructively express themselves if they are to discover a joy in living.

In recent years the great upsurge in do-it-yourself activities reflects the necessity for the individual to discover ways to be creative. Perhaps this is due to the fact that many individuals in earning a living seem to find themselves engaged in routine activities that are devoid of opportunities to express their own individuality.

For any of us to have a fuller enjoyment of living, regardless of our age, we must discover some way in which to express the creative urge of Life within us. It is never too soon or too late to start!

∞

Right Action

Right action means that every legitimate and constructive purpose you have in mind shall be successfully executed. It means that you will know what to do, how to think, how to act, how to proceed. You definitely know that if your thought is in accord with the Divine Nature it actually is the Law of God enforcing Itself in your experience. Hence, there is nothing in you or around you which can limit your constructive thought. The Power of this Law is within you and the action which results from this Power produces harmony, peace, joy and success.

SAY: I know that in this consciousness of the Divine Nature is the supply for my every need—physical, mental or spiritual—and I accept that supply in deepest gratitude.

I am thankful that this is the way Life fulfills my needs, through the doorway of my inner self, and I am thankful that I know how to use this perfect Law.

I come to this great Fountain of Supply, in the very center of my being, to absorb that for which I have need, mentally and physically, and I am filled with the sense of the reality of that which I desire.

I permit this awareness to flow into my world of thought and action, knowing that it brings peace, harmony and order all around me.

There arises within me renewed faith in the limitless resources of the Divine Presence, the perfect Law, and there is now right action in all my ways.

Mental Records

We often become tired of hearing the same record being played over and over again. Of course it is easy to stop the record and find ourselves at peace again. But what about our own thoughts, those ideas that keep chasing themselves round and round in our minds? With regularity the same pattern of thought keeps repeating itself with no end in sight. And the tune that is being played is one that we definitely don't like.

It has been said that a neurotic thought pattern constantly repeats itself. Such neurotic thought patterns usually involve feelings of hate, fear, anxiety and guilt. If there is such a thing as perpetual motion it exists when we find ourselves caught in the merry-go-round of our own negative thinking.

Usually we sit back and listen to these tunes by the hour, becoming emotionally and physically exhausted. Then we wind up in the doctor's office. And in nine cases out of ten, if the doctor is honest, he or she will tell us that he or she can alleviate some of the aches and pains our mental spree has caused us, but can't prevent them from returning. If we would only realize it, we can do with our minds just what we would do with our record player when such a thing occurs. We can change the record.

There are many mental records we can play which are enjoyable and beneficial, but it may take a little time to discover them. The record of hate needs to be replaced with one of love, fear with confidence, anxiety with faith and guilt with forgiveness. After awhile, when our mind starts to play a pattern of thought we don't like, we will discover we can automatically change it and play a more harmonious one.

∞

Freedom from Fear

To have your heart be without fear is to have implicit confidence in the good, the enduring and the true. *Fear* is the only thing of which to be afraid. It is not the host encamped against you, nor the confusion around you, that you need to fear; it is the lack of confidence in the good alone which should concern you. Through inner spiritual vision you know that good alone is permanent and all else is transitory. You know that right finally dissolves everything opposed to it. The power of Spirit is supreme over every antagonist. Therefore, you should cherish no fear, and when you neither fear nor hate, you come to understand the unity of Life.

SAY: I realize that fear is not Godlike, since it contradicts the Divine Presence, repudiates limitless Love and denies infinite Good.

Fear is neither person, place nor thing; it is merely an impostor that I have believed in; I have entertained it so long that it seems as if it really were something.

Today I repudiate all fear.

I renounce all thoughts of hate.

I enter into conscious union with the Spirit.

I accept Good as supreme, positive and absolute.

With joy I enter into the activities of the day, without regret I remember the events of yesterday, and with confidence I look forward to tomorrow, for today my heart is without fear.

We are all bound, tied hand and foot, by our very freedom; our free will binds us; but as free will enables us to create the conditions which externally limit us, so it can uncreate or dissolve them.

It is not enough to say that we attract what we think; we become what we think, and what we become we attract.

Through an inherent Law of Mind we increase whatever we praise. Praise yourself from weakness to strength, from ignorance to intelligence, from poverty into abundance.

Such is the power of right thinking that it cancels and erases everything unlike itself.

—FROM *THE SCRAPBOOK* OF ERNEST HOLMES

II

The Life You Live

Living is a very personal matter. Nobody can do it for you. Others can offer much advice and endless suggestions as to what you should do and how to do it. Then there are the constant suggestions you make to yourself out of your past successes and failures. However, in the last analysis whatever you have come to know resolves itself into your own mental concepts, colored and enhanced by your own emotional and physical nature.

You are you. What you are and what you are to become is the result of an inner motivation which you alone have established. Unknowingly you have perhaps been directing yourself in a direction other than that in which you desired to go.

As you come to understand the way your mind is creative, new vistas of living will open up for you. That greater experience and appreciation of life can only be yours by first establishing an inner awareness that it is yours.

Inner Space

The imagination of the whole country is captured by the probes that are being sent into outer space. In an article dealing with the space age the author commented that "the simplest and most basic motivation of the drive into space is man's enduring and insatiable drive to explore and know his environment. Space is a challenge simply because, like Mount Everest, it is there."

The infinity that lies outside of us is marvelous to contemplate. But the amazing thing is that the infinity that lies within us is yet but little realized. Outer space should be explored. But should not inner space, the realm of our thought, also be subject to more intensive investigation?

The very thing that enables us to explore outer space, our ability to think, is for the most part the greatest of enigmas. A considerable amount of investigation, research and measurement of the brain has been done. But the brain is only the instrument for thought. As for thought itself, that thing which creates beautiful poetry, great art, engineering wonders, and experiences love and affection, little is known about it. Yet it is the most important thing that we have; it is what makes us human.

In times to come scientific savants will devote more attention to this nebulous, intangible thing we call our mind. But in the meantime, this inner space is something that we can investigate for ourselves. Each person can become a scientific researcher. The equipment with which we work is our own thought. And the results of our experiments can have measurable effects in our everyday living.

∞

Divine Power

Everything in nature is an individualization of one coordinating Life—one Presence and one Law of being. The mind has become so filled with that which contradicts this that even the Truth has to await your recognition. You must learn to become consciously aware of the Divine Presence and the Divine Power; the wholeness of Truth, of Love and of Reason. Instead of dwelling on negative thoughts, cause your mind to dwell on peace and joy. Discover the power of the invisible Spirit that is working in and through you now, at this very moment. Lay hold of this realization with complete certainty.

SAY: I know that I am a perfect being now, living under perfect conditions today.

Knowing that Spirit alone is real, I know that there is one Power which acts and reacts in my experience, in my body and in my thought, for my good.

I know that this recognition establishes, through Law, harmony in my experience, prosperity, a sense of happiness, peace, health and joy.

Today I hold communion with this invisible Presence which peoples the world with the manifestations of Its life, Its light and Its love.

I withdraw the veil which hides my real self and draw close to the Spirit within, that is in everything and in everyone.

I accept everything that belongs to this Spirit.

I claim everything that partakes of Its nature.

Mental Health

There has been a great deal of talk during the last few years about mental health. It sounds like a very desirable thing to have, but just what it is and what we as individuals can do about it seems to be a little nebulous.

For this reason it was very gratifying to encounter the concise statement of W. W. Bauer, M.D., Director of Health Education for the American Medical Association. He said that mental health concerns itself with everyone's relationship to ourselves, to those about us and to the conditions around us. This has a strangely familiar sound, if memory serves us right. A long time ago a definition of religion was encountered which went like this: The purpose of religion is to establish everyone's proper relationship to ourselves, to our neighbors, to the world in which we live and to our God or Maker.

It is this fourth point which the present-day mental health program seems to have unintentionally overlooked. But is it not possible that the mental health program for the individual, or for society as a whole, may succeed or fail depending upon what one thinks about God and one's relationship to God? Time and time again it has been pointed out by men and women of science and religion that our entire thought and action springs from our innermost convictions, and that it is fundamental to the nature of humankind to develop a religious attitude, whether it be constructive or destructive to our welfare.

Our relationship to our Maker is something each one of us needs to clarify for ourself in a manner that is intelligent and emotionally sound. Then the problems arising in the three areas of interest to the mental health program will automatically take care of themselves.

∞

Perfect Patterns

When you go up onto a mountain in your consciousness and lift your thought above the confusion of everything that seems to be disconnected and dissociated, you become unified with the pattern of spiritual Cause back of all things. In psychosomatic medicine, and all forms of psychological adjustment, the suggestion of a universal pattern back of things, a pattern which in itself and of itself must be perfect, is automatically being dealt with. It is no idle statement to affirm the perfection of God in all things, manifesting in and through each and every thing in a unique way.

SAY: I affirm the perfection of the Divine Pattern at the center of my being.

Realizing Its reality, I permit Its essence to flow through me, claiming it as my very own.

Believing in Its wholeness, perfection and right action, I know that everything in my experience conforms to Its nature.

Accepting Its peace, I am calm.

Expressing Its love, I am unified with life.

Believing in Its power, with childlike faith I accept the authority of Its action in my everyday affairs.

Today I declare the presence and activity of Spirit in that which I am, in my relationships with others and in my contacts with the world about me.

Problems

We all seem to have our share of problems of one kind or another which we don't like and want to get rid of. But in trying to get rid of problems an interesting question arises: To what extent are we creating for ourselves the very things we want no part of?

A study based on father-mother-child groups at the University Psychology Clinic, University of Illinois, revealed that to a large extent the problems parents are confronted with in their children are the result of their own problems and maladjustments. In other words, the parents are creating the problems they are trying to solve!

Most of the difficulties we encounter in life do not just descend upon us out of "nowhere." Without realizing it, in some way we create them, or attract them to us, through the way we think, feel or act. We can also get rid of our problems in the same way!

Regardless of the difficulty that confronts us, the first thing we should do is to find out what we are thinking, for this is the factor controlling the way we feel and act. Are we constantly thinking about the problem, or seeking its answer? Is our thinking increasing or reducing the size of the difficulty? Problems have a habit of appearing or disappearing according to a causative factor which may be resolved into a process of thought.

Instead of considering a problem as a thing which exists entirely outside ourselves, if we take the time to carefully examine our thinking we will no doubt find that the difficulty had its source within us. Unless we learn to think with discretion and care we will find ourselves battling real live problems into which our thoughts have grown.

∞

Solutions

God is the Presence and the Power that knows all things and can do all things. And if you will but take your personal problem to that high place in your own consciousness and feel that the answer takes the place of the problem, then the problem will be solved. You need to know that there is nothing in you that can keep this from happening; that there is no doubt or limitation in your mind. You should feel that the answer is established in your consciousness and will make itself known to you, right now, in your present experience. To find the solution to a problem, let go of it, and definitely expect the answer.

SAY. I do know that my every thought and act is governed by a superior Intelligence.

There is something in me that knows what to do.

It not only knows what to do, but It compels me to act upon what It knows.

Therefore, everything I ought to do, I shall do; anything I ought to know, I shall know.

Whatever seeming problems or difficulties may confront me, with complete assurance I accept Divine guidance.

Right now there is the right solution for my every problem.

There is an inner, quiet flowing stream of Life that carries me surely and safely to my proper destination and accomplishment of my every good purpose.

The Dangerous Age

Certain ailments seem to appear when a person reaches a particular age, but an interesting question in this connection is whether it is the age reached, or the attitude toward it, that is the cause of the difficulty.

Dr. John L. Parks of George Washington University, in his gynecologic studies, has found that many of the problems of women over fifty can be solved with psychology rather than surgery. Many of the complications that he encounters in patients at this age are not necessarily of organic origin. He has also found that there is increased happiness when an individual finds new expressions of useful creativity.

From this point of view most any age could be considered a dangerous age. Most every individual bogs down physically and is possessed of many different ailments and symptoms when he or she is unable to find a vital and creative interest. Regardless of age, the individual who is bored, frustrated and uncreative is the one who is beset with all kinds of physical problems. Then the main focus of attention becomes the physical problem and this only tends to increase the difficulty.

A lazy mind creates a sluggish body which seldom functions properly. But the person who is able to discover ways to express himself or herself in a creative, constructive manner is happy mentally, and healthy physically. One of the greatest vitality tonics is a mental attitude that is interested and enthused about doing something that is productive and allows an opportunity for self-expression.

A dangerous period can be encountered at any age. It is not the calendar, but how we think, that determines how old we are or feel.

∞

Creative Action

When Jesus spoke of being "lifted up from the earth" he meant that that which is human about you must consciously become united with the Divine. In ancient writings the earth stood for the lowest form of life, while heaven represented the highest. Therefore, being lifted up from the earth means uniting with heaven. This daily lifting up of your thought is necessary if you wish to so unite yourself and everything you are doing with the Divine spiritual Power that flows through you and into all your acts.

SAY: I now turn to the Spirit within me.

I know that It is close to me, It is what I am, and It governs my life in harmony and in peace.

I know that through me It brings joy and happiness to everyone I meet.

Through the Power of this indwelling Spirit I am a blessing to myself and others.

I lift up my whole mind to the realization that the Spirit of God is within me and that this perfect Spirit is my real self.

I invite the Spirit to direct my thoughts and acts, and I accept that It is now doing so.

I expect new ideas to stimulate my imagination and direct me into new ways of doing things.

I expect new circumstances and situations.

The action of Divine Intelligence within me impels me to act for the greatest benefit of myself and others.

Do You Like Your Job?

A survey made by the Gallup Poll revealed the somewhat startling fact that nearly half of the people are unhappy in the work they are doing. This is an alarmingly high percentage and discloses a situation which should be looked into. But what would one look into—the job or the person?

Could it be that half of the things that are to be done in this country of ours are tasks that no one would like? It hardly seems possible because a great many people are happy at what they are doing while others would be extremely unhappy at the same task. A fair question to ask ourselves is whether or not we would be happy at any kind of job, or are we allergic to work?

Whatever we can do about work we dislike, we have to do to ourselves. We are the source of our own unhappiness. It is the way we react to our work, not what the work does to us. If we cannot in some way find it possible to be happy at the work we are now doing we never will find work that can make us happy.

We all have to work because we all have to eat, and we may as well be happy in the process. The food tastes so much better that way. Regardless of what we are doing let us find something interesting in it; something that can make it enjoyable, even if it applies only to a part of our activity. We have to start to like something or we will never learn to like anything. We have to be able to lift ourselves out of that 50 percent class who resent and dislike their work. Putting it bluntly, it is plain nonsense to allow ourselves to be miserable more than half the time we are awake. When we can learn to like the job we are now doing, we will be able to find one we will like even more.

∞

Nonresistance

Gandhi built his whole philosophy of life around the theory of nonviolence. An ancient Chinese sage said that all things are possible to those who can perfectly practice inaction. Jesus said to "resist not evil." Surely some truth must be contained in these simple thoughts. If so, and if there is a spiritual transcendence of consciousness which dissolves solid facts, then you ought to learn about it and use it.

Think of an iceberg, with the sun's rays falling on it. Soon it will dissolve. That which was an obstruction becomes liquid. Perhaps that is the meaning of spiritual transcendence, inner awareness, the power of nonviolence. The great, the good and the wise have known this. But too often that which is not liked is resisted rather than being overcome.

SAY: Today I practice nonresistance.

Disregarding everything that seems to contradict the Reality in which I believe, I affirm that Reality is operating in my life.

Turning resolutely from everything that denies the good I wish to experience, I affirm that good.

In the midst of fear I proclaim faith.

At the center of uncertainty I proclaim conviction.

In the midst of want I proclaim abundance.

Where unhappiness seems to exist I announce joy.

There is no situation or condition that resists these transcendent thoughts, for they proclaim the omnipotence of God, and the Divine guidance of the Mind that can accomplish all things.

Success

There is an old familiar saying that "Nothing succeeds like success." To this rather obvious idea perhaps we should add the not-so-obvious one that "We always succeed." What is meant by "success"? It may be defined as the fulfillment, accomplishment or achievement of those ideas which preeminently occupy one's thinking.

Consider the individuals who have had success all their lives—they have found joy, happiness, wealth, health and are still enjoying them at a ripe old age. Others also had success—they have never had a dime, their health has been poor, their family life was a flop and everything is still going on in a dreary way. Everyone has been successful in experiencing those things which they expected to happen to them!

Perhaps it might be wise to take a look at the state of our own affairs. Are they all that we could wish them to be? Or, on the other hand, are they just what we expect them to be? There is a vast difference.

Inasmuch as we always have success, we should be more careful in what we are successful at. Are we successful in experiencing what we want, or what we don't want? This brings us to the question: What do we think about most of the time—the "wants" or the "don't wants"? Here lies the big secret of why some people appear successful in experiencing the good things in life while others appear not to have been around when they were passed out. The good things of life are always being passed around. But apparently the only way to have your share of them is to continually mentally accept them and not reject them. You can't have what you refuse to take.

∞

Words Have Power

You are either attracting or repelling according to your mental attitudes. You are either identifying yourself with lack or with abundance, with love and friendship or with indifference. You cannot keep from attracting into your experience that which corresponds to the sum total of your states of consciousness. This law of attraction and repulsion works automatically. It is like the law of reflection— the reflection corresponds to the object held before a mirror.

How careful, then, you should be to guard your thoughts, not only seeing to it that you keep them free from doubt and fear—accepting only the good—but, equally, you should consciously repel every thought which denies that good.

SAY: I know that my acceptance of only good in my experience penetrates any unbelief in my mind, casts out fear, removes doubt and clears away obstacles, permitting that which is enduring, perfect and true to be realized.

I have complete faith and acceptance that all the worthwhile ideas I now affirm will be fulfilled as I have believed.

I do everything with a sense of reliance upon the Law of Mind; therefore I know that my word shall not return unto me void.

I accept this word and rejoice in it.

I expect complete and successful fulfillment of my thoughts of increased good which I now establish.

Calculated Thought

When we come into this world we possess a great deal more wisdom and intelligence than we ever give ourselves credit for. The wisdom the body has in maintaining normal functioning and continual repair of itself does and probably always will defy our full comprehension. Even more incomprehensible is the mind, the process of thought, which starts out functioning more or less on an instinctive level but which seems to have no upper limit of development.

Some say the mind operates much like an electronic computer of gigantic proportions. In many respects they may be right, but on the other hand computers require operators, so apparently we have *something* within us which is over, above and beyond the mere mechanical operation of billions of nerves in our brain.

A computer always comes up with an answer that is directly related to the facts, figures and information that is fed into it. Whether the answer is liked or not does not come into the picture at all.

The things we do, the way we feel, the relationships we maintain are the inevitable consequences of the ideas and information we supply our minds. Not only are our conscious thoughts acted upon, but there is that memory storehouse we have been placing things in for years that plays a part in any result we secure. When we don't like the experiences we encounter we are prone to lay all the blame on conditions outside ourselves, forgetting entirely that for the most part no other answer is possible from what our mind has had to work with. However, we can always start to produce different results in our experience by feeding our minds different data which will provide us with more usable and beneficial answers.

∞

Affirmation

Through affirmative thinking you are able to clear your mind of negative thoughts, fears and doubts. This you must come to do if you are to become aware of the Presence, Peace and Harmony of God that is within and around you. All the good that you desire awaits your acceptance of it. But you cannot experience it while you deny it. The key to right thinking and right living is the steady affirmative pattern of thought that only God's Good enters your life.

SAY: God is all Power, all Presence and all Peace.

I now let go of all fear, doubt and confusion, and turn my thought and attention to the belief that only good is my experience.

I have faith to believe that God is Perfect, and that nothing unlike that Perfection could be His desire for His creation.

Peace and happiness, joy and contentment always walk with me.

I am surrounded by Divine right action and It flows through my every experience.

I patiently brush aside every doubt or fear that enters my mind and resolutely accept only the wonderful things of the kingdom of God here and now.

God is all the Power there is, all the Presence there is and all the Life there is, and only that which is of the nature of God enters my life.

Unhappiness Is a Habit

As much as we might not like to admit it, much of the unhappiness that we encounter in daily living we have sought out. There seems to be a perverse streak running through us that takes a particular delight in wallowing in the mire of despondency, talking about our troubles and indulging in self-pity. Listen to much of your own conversation and pay particular attention to what others talk about. You'll be surprised at what you hear. Toil, trouble, headaches and heartaches for the most part, and only a few expressions of joy, happiness and an enthusiasm for living.

Nobody ever thrived mentally or physically by dwelling on the negative aspects of living. As much as we might seemingly enjoy such self-indulgence, we are blinding ourselves to the "real" joy of living. Perhaps we have never realized that a better existence is even possible.

With a little effort we can untie the tangled knots of our thoughts. And even though we might be skeptical about what we might encounter we can turn ourselves around and head in another direction mentally and just try sampling the results of a different pattern of thinking.

Certainly we are going to encounter some unpleasantries during the day. But also during the day some favorable things will happen to us and there will be pleasant encounters with others. As the day progresses, and at the end of the day, let us have our thoughts dwell on the pleasant events. We can discover a new joy in living—happiness rather than unhappiness.

∞

Life's Song

You are part of the universal Mind, one with the universal Substance. You live, move and have your being in pure Spirit. All the abundance, the power and the harmony of this Spirit exist at the center of your being. You experience this good in such degree as you accept, believe in and feel it. As you enter into life, feeling the Divine Presence in everything, more and more you will hear a Song of Joy singing at the center of your being. You have only to be still and listen to this Song of Life, for It is always there.

SAY: Knowing that the Divine Presence is always closer to me than my very breath, I have nothing to fear.

I feel this loving protection around me.

I know that the Song of Joy, of Love and of Peace, is forever chanting Its hymn of praise and beauty at the center of my being, therefore I tune out of my mind all unhappy and negative ideas.

I direct my thought to the sunshine of life, to brightness and laughter, to the joyous presence of radiant Spirit.

I lay aside all anxiety, all striving and let Divine Love operate through me into my affairs.

Joyfully I anticipate greater abundance, more success and a deeper peace.

Joy wells up within my mind, and Life sings Its song of ecstasy in my heart.

Your Most Important Diet

For one reason or another it seems that a majority of our population is vitally concerned about some kind of diet. There is the continual question of what to eat or not to eat. In actual practice not too much is ever done about the food that is eaten, but the subject does provide endless material for conversation. So we find that mostly a diet winds up as food for thought rather than food for the body.

This of course immediately brings up the subject of just what kind of food we are feeding our minds other than the subject matter of what kind of food we should feed our stomachs. We are continually pouring into our minds all kinds of ideas for it to consume, without any consideration as to their value. Sometimes some of the ideas dumped into the hopper of thought are pleasant, easily consumed and very beneficial. Then there are other times when we literally find ourselves with a serious problem of mental indigestion.

We should bear in mind that the ideas we mentally absorb are the ones that control the nature of our experience. If our mental diet is one consisting of ideas of failure, that is what the body of our experience becomes. On the other hand, a continuing supply of ideas of success will make everything in our life vital and prosperous.

The best way to change undesirable situations is to completely change our mental diet. We need to switch our brand of ideas from what we don't want to what we do want. We are our own best doctor for prescribing how this is to be done. But we need to be good patients and consistently take what we have prescribed. It may take a little time before results are noticed, but definite improvements will be forthcoming.

∞

Spiritual Supply

Spirit fills all space and animates every form, therefore Spirit is the true actor in everything. But Spirit can only act for you by acting through you. This means simply that God can only give you what you take. As you daily enter into your Divine inheritance, with your thought and heart, you are entering into the realm of absolute Causation. Completely believe that from this secret place of the Most High within you there shall be projected an objective manifestation of your every legitimate desire. Are you really accepting abundance? Is your thought really animating your experience with the idea of plenty? Are you affirming that Divine Substance is forever flowing to you as supply?

SAY: Today I praise the abundance of all things.

I animate everything with the idea of abundance.

I am remembering only the good; I am expecting more good; I am experiencing good.

I acknowledge that the Spirit is working everywhere.

I give thanks that the right action of Spirit is flowing into my experience in ever-increasing volume.

There is that within me that sees, knows and understands this truth, which completely accepts it.

There is good enough to go around.

Therefore I do not withhold that good from myself or others, but constantly proclaim spiritual abundance is forever flowing to each and all as supply.

I now accept as mine all that is needed to make my life a joyous experience.

Internal Weather

The state of the weather is probably the most talked about of all subjects, except how we feel, and when we talk about the weather we are indirectly telling others how we feel. If the days are hot some people love it, others complain endlessly. Some are miserable when it is cold, while others are invigorated. Even though we are able to accommodate ourselves to many of the vicissitudes of the weather through clothing and heating or cooling equipment, we react emotionally in a favorable or unfavorable manner. So when we come right down to it, what bothers us is our internal weather.

Too often we forget that weather, whether or not it is the kind we like, is a vital necessity for making the earth a place to live on. In fact only through changes was it at all possible for life to even get started.

If we think of our earth as something that is alive, something that breathes with the great masses of circulating air about it; that nourishes itself with a terrific circulatory system of water being evaporated from the oceans and deposited on parched soil; that rebuilds itself through an endless process of breaking down and rebuilding its structural system through deterioration of rock to sand to soil, and the reformation of rock; that through its ceaseless sequence of seasons prevents stagnation, then we find that all kinds of weather are necessary.

What we should get disturbed about is not the weather but that we let ourselves be emotionally wrought up by those climatic changes which enable us to live on this earth.

∞

Peace

A basic Harmony must exist at the center of everything or the Universe Itself would be a chaos. You already know this and believe it; now you are going to act upon it. You are not only going to believe in it, you are going to act as though it were true, because it is true. There is peace at the center of your being—a peace that can be felt through the day and in the cool of the evening when you have turned from your labor and the first star shines in the soft light of the sky. It broods over the earth quietly, tenderly, as a mother watches over her child.

SAY: In this peace that holds me so gently I find strength and protection from all fear or anxiety.

It is the peace of God in which I feel the love of a Holy Presence.

I am so conscious of this love, this protection, that every sense of fear slips away from me as mist fades in the morning light.

I see good in everything, God personified in all people, Life manifest in every event.

Spirit is not separate from persons or events; I see that It unites everything with Itself, vitalizing all with the energy of Its own being, creating everything through Its own Divine imagination, surrounding everything with peace and quiet and calm.

I am one with this deep, abiding peace.

I know that all is well.

Expectancy always speeds progress, anticipation of "Better Yet To Come" helps to dissolve the load of unbelief which we now carry with us. We must learn to increase our consciousness. Nothing is too good to be true. God's perfection is already an ever-present reality, but as far as we are concerned it waits to be perceived, and only as much good can come to us as we mentally accept. If we have condemned any particular organ or function of our body, we should not only cease doing this, but we should cancel our condemnation.

—FROM *THE SCRAPBOOK* OF ERNEST HOLMES

III

Your Mental and Spiritual Health

There are many aspects of health, and you, like everyone else, at one time or another are greatly concerned about them. Health in any respect is not a thing that can be earned as a reward; neither can it be bought. This does not mean that there are not many aids and much assistance of which you can avail yourself.

There is one thing that needs to be remembered: Life is a dynamic animating Force. It is this Force which continually seeks to express and flow through you. No one can explain what It is, or how It works. But that It exists there is no doubt, for otherwise there would not be a you.

There are many ways by which you may increase or impede Its action. The least recognized, and yet probably the most vital, is the power of your own thought. In your own mind, to a large degree, rests the ability to deny or accept and use the continuing flow of the dynamic Force of Life which created you in the first place.

Your Welcome Sign

We all like to think that we are friendly. We like to meet new people, and friends are welcome at our home. We enjoy new experiences and generally like life to be a continuing new experience. But just how big is the welcome sign that hangs over our heads? Do we feel we have many uninvited guests in our experience, not realizing we have blindly scattered our invitations in every direction?

It is certain that we consciously or unconsciously invite many of our aches, pains and illnesses. The person who is happy, joyous and gets a kick out of living is the person who is usually free from sickness; the opposite type of person is the one who has the most physical complaints. If we are grouchy, unpleasant, irritable, resentful and fearsome, are not these the welcome signs we hand out inviting in similar irritating factors which contribute to our physical discomfort?

We find ourselves confronted with the question of whether or not we can afford to think in the manner that we so often do. We often complain about having caught this or that ailment, little realizing that we actually have gone out of our way to catch it by hanging out a certain type of welcome sign.

Our thoughts are like bait in a trap. We can catch most anything we want by varying the kind of bait that we use. What kind of bait are you using? What are you welcoming into your experience? If you do not like the kind of situations you are entertaining in your experience, change the sign over the door of your thoughts, stop sending out invitations in a haphazard manner. You have the ability and right to be discriminating in the life you live.

∞

READER/CUSTOMER CARE SURVEY

We care about your opinions. Please take a moment to fill out this Reader Survey card and mail it back to us.
As a special **"thank you"** we'll send you exciting news about interesting books and a valuable **Gift Certificate.**

Please PRINT using ALL CAPS

Name |___|___|___|___|___|___|___|___|___|___|___|___|___|___|___|___|___|___|
First   MI. |___| Last Name

Address |___|___|___|___|___|___|___|___|___|___|___|___|___|___|___|___|___|

City |___|___|___|___|___|___|___|___| ST |___| Zip |___|___|___|___|___| — |___|___|___|___|

Phone # (|___|___|___|) |___|___|___| — |___|___|___|___| Fax # (|___|___|___|) |___|___|___| — |___|___|___|___|

Email |___|___|___|___|___|___|___|___|___|___|___|___|___|___|___|___|___|___|

(1) Gender:
___Female   ___Male

(2) Age:
___12 or under   ___40-59
___13-19   ___60+
___20-39

(3) Marital Status
___Married
___Single
___Divorced/Widowed

(4) Did you receive this book as a gift?
___Yes   ___No

(5) How many Health Communications books have you bought or read?
___1   ___2-4   ___5+

(6) How did you find out about this book?
Please fill in ONE.
1) ___ Recommendation
2) ___ Store Display
3) ___ Bestseller List
4) ___ Online
5) ___ Advertisement
6) ___ Catalog/Mailing
7) ___ Interview/Review (TV, Radio, Print)

(7) Where do you usually buy books?
Please fill in your top TWO choices.
1) ___ Bookstore
2) ___ Religious Bookstore
3) ___ Online
4) ___ Book Club/Mail Order
5) ___ Price Club (Costco, Sam's Club, etc.)

(9) What subjects do you enjoy reading about most? Rank only *FIVE*. *Use 1 for your favorite, 2 for second favorite, etc.*

	1	2	3	4	5
1) Parenting/Family	○	○	○	○	○
2) Relationships	○	○	○	○	○
3) Recovery/Addictions	○	○	○	○	○
4) Health/Nutrition	○	○	○	○	○
5) Christianity	○	○	○	○	○
6) Spirituality/Inspiration	○	○	○	○	○
7) Business Self-Help	○	○	○	○	○
8) Teen Issues	○	○	○	○	○
9) Sports	○	○	○	○	○

(14) What attracts you most to a book?
(Please rank 1-4 in order of preference.)

	1	2	3	4
1) Title	○	○	○	○
2) Cover Design	○	○	○	○
3) Author	○	○	○	○

FOLD HERE

Comments:

Accept Only Good

The good in which you believe can triumph over every evil you have experienced. You have a silent partnership with the Infinite. This partnership has never been dissolved; it never can be. You are to have implicit confidence in your own ability, knowing that it is the nature of thought to externalize itself in your health and affairs, knowing that you are the thinker. You are going to turn resolutely from every sense of lack, want and limitation, and declare that the perfect Law of God is operating in, for and through you.

SAY: I have complete confidence in my knowledge and understanding of the Law of Mind.

I not only know what the Law is, I know how to use It.

I know that I shall obtain definite results through the use of It.

Knowing this, having confidence in my ability to use the Law and using It daily for specific purposes, gradually I build up an unshakable faith, both in the Law and the possibility of demonstrating It.

Therefore, today I declare that my thoughts shall only be affirmative, positive and constructive.

Today I believe that "underneath are the everlasting arms," and I rest in this Divine assurance and this Divine security.

I know, not only that all is well with my mind and my body—all is well with my affairs.

How Old Are You?

Birthdays have a habit of coming around and as the years pass, they seem to come more frequently. But regardless of what the calendar might say there is still a lot of truth in the statement that we are as young as we feel. This leaves us with the problem of discovering just what it is that determines how we feel. What is it that provides us with a feeling of vitality, well-being and a continuing enjoyment of living?

Milton Golin, writing in the *Journal of the American Medical Association,* reported on a survey of senior citizens. He pointed out that there is much to fortify the medical conviction that sustained growth and vigor depend, to a large degree, on some positive motive for living. Without such a motive a person of thirty-five might be old, while an older person with a motive for living might be young.

It is obvious that Life is always active, creative and constructive. We are part of Life and not separate from It, so it behooves us to be similarly active. We have to have something to be active about, some positive, vital, productive interest. In other words, we have to provide ourselves with some reason to stay alive.

We may often find ourselves, seemingly, at the end of our rope. But there is a lot more rope there if we learn to open our minds and start to think a little. Some people may find a vital interest in building bridges, others in growing geraniums or caring for grandchildren, while still others in their maturity can offer wisdom in meeting the problems of living to those younger. Regardless of the calendar, there is a reason for living, a positive motive. You can find it, and will find it, if you stop blocking the flow of Life through you.

∞

Renewal

Your body, every part of it, is a manifestation of Spirit. Its perfect pattern in the Mind of God cannot deteriorate. This instant the Divine vitality that is constantly flowing through you takes form in the likeness of perfect, whole, complete cells. Every cell of your body is strong and healthy, filled with life and vitality, strength and cleanliness. Your body, Spirit in form, knows no time, knows no degree; it knows only to express fully, instantaneously.

SAY: I recognize that Spirit is within me and It is that which I am.

I let this recognition of my indwelling Divinity flow through my entire consciousness.

I let it reach down into the very depths of my being.

I rejoice in my Divinity.

I am now made vigorous, robust and mentally creative.

I am fortified with God's perfection and right action.

I am healthy and able-bodied.

The Life of God is my life.

The Strength of God is my strength.

The Mind of God is my mind.

Every breath I draw fills me with perfection and vital-izes, upbuilds and renews every cell of my body.

I am born in Spirit and of Spirit, and I am Spirit made manifest this instant.

Healthy Convictions

For a long time medical researchers have been emphasizing the relationship between stress and bodily conditions. Stress, which includes a wide range of mental and emotional reactions to life situations, can be a conditioning or causative factor responsible for many of our physical ailments. But often we are unable to identify the source of serious stress. Perhaps it is a wolf in sheep's clothing!

This is what medical men and religious authorities are discovering. It has long been presumed that a person's religion is a source of strength and a refuge providing peace of mind. But all too frequently just the reverse is true. No religious beliefs can be said to be good or bad for a person, rather it is the individual's reactions to the beliefs that may be good or bad. Our religion should provide us with a healthy, joyous attitude toward life and living. It should also establish within us a wholesome relationship between ourselves, our fellow humans and our Maker. When it does not provide us with a sense of well-being, but instead instills fear, apprehension and anxiety, we find that religion then becomes a source of stress.

Regardless of what one's professed religious convictions are, they need to be examined carefully. Are they providing joy and a sense of well-being, or are they corrosives eating away the vitality of life? We need to decide for ourselves what beliefs fill our needs and are right for us and not let them be determined by another or by family tradition. What is right for one person is not necessarily right for another. We each have our own life to live. Basically religion is an intense inner personal experience between ourselves and that Power greater than we are, and the channel of communication is our own thought.

∞

Understanding

The Spirit of God is an undivided and indivisible Wholeness. It fills all time with Its presence and permeates space with the activity of Its thought. Your endeavor, then, is not so much to find God as it is to realize God's Presence and to understand that this Presence is always with you. Nothing can be nearer to you than that which is the very essence of your being. Your outward search for God culminates in the greatest of all possible discoveries—finding God at the center of your own being. Life flows up from within you.

SAY: I know that my search is over.
I am consciously aware of the Presence of the Spirit.
I have discovered the great Reality.
I am awake to the realization of this Presence.
There is but One Life.
Today I see It reflected in every form, back of every countenance, moving through every act.
I know that the Divine Presence is everywhere.
I salute the good in everything.
I recognize God-Life responding to me from every person I meet, in every event that transpires, in every circumstance in my experience.
I feel the warmth and color of this Divine Presence forevermore pressing against me, forevermore welling up from within me—the wellspring of Eternal Being, present yesterday, today, tomorrow and always.

Help Yourself

After attending a meeting of medical evangelists, a reporter started his article with a statement to the effect that the doctor who today discounts the value of prayer in the treatment of physical ailments will soon be as out of date as the doctor of a hundred years ago who laughed at the use of ether.

Although it may be some time before the medical profession as a whole comes to the point of acknowledging and accepting the usefulness of prayer in the treatment of physical ailments, there are many, many individual doctors who realize the necessity of affirmative prayer in the recovery and maintenance of good health.

This whole trend is one that patients will not particularly like. They would much rather the doctor give them a pill to correct all that is wrong with them and let that be the end of the matter. This would be the easy way out, but it does not always work. For a doctor to tell patients that they will have to change their way of thinking, that they will have to start thinking in an affirmative rather than negative manner, means that they will have to do some consistent constructive thinking–praying.

Prayer is a process of thinking in a certain way, so it may be considered that every thought is in some respect a prayer, a creative factor in our experience. From this point of view it can be seen that our prayers or thoughts may be directly responsible for our experience of either good or bad health.

What are you doing through the way you think that retards or promotes your experience of good health?

∞

Wholeness

Regardless of what negative condition may exist in your physical body, there is in the Mind of God a pattern of perfection for your body. Otherwise it never could have been created to begin with, or sustained and renewed. Your life is of God. Your health is the expression of the Perfection of Spirit within you. As you recognize that there is a River of Life within you, which flows from the eternal Source of all Life, you need to open your mind and accept the full influx of Its life-giving Power.

SAY: I now affirm that every organ, action and function of my physical body is animated by the living Spirit.

There is one perfect Mind directing my thoughts, one complete Wholeness sustaining my being, one Divine circulation flowing through me.

By day and by night I realize that the Divine Life that is flowing through me is renewing every cell of my body after the image of Its own perfection. I give thanks for this silent Power which sustains me, and I say to my own mind: "You are to believe in this Power. You are to accept It. You are to let It flow through you, for you are one with It. There is no other power, no other presence and no other life; therefore, all the Power there is, all the Presence there is, and all the Life there is, is sustaining you now and will continue to sustain you."

Old Wives' Tales

There are many sayings which fall into the category of what might be termed "old wives' tales." These are homey words of seeming wisdom which may or may not have a bit of truth in them. However, there is always the possibility that we often laugh at them because we do not want to face up to the truth they do contain.

One such tale concerns the idea that an expectant mother should be kept free from all worry and anxiety. In more recent years it has come to be looked upon as nothing more than a kindly gesture and due consideration for the condition she is in. The amazing thing is that the pendulum has again swung back and the idea is in vogue as a necessity. Medical research shows that the birth of normal children, to a large extent, depends on the lack of stress in the mother during pregnancy.

If stress, worry and anxiety can affect the normalcy of a child yet to be born, it would only be logical to assume that such states of mind also affect those of us who are already born. Of course this is well known in the field of psychosomatic medicine, and many of us are aware of what such destructive attitudes can do to our health.

It is only normal and natural that in the process of everyday living we encounter stresses, strains and anxieties. If we did not, we would not be alive, we would be the proverbial bump on a log. The thing to be watched, apparently, is to what degree we are permitting ourselves to get mentally and emotionally embroiled in these destructive attitudes which have such dire consequences. It is not that we don't know what our thinking is doing to our health, but rather that we do not go to the trouble of doing anything about our thinking.

∞

The Power Within

It is possible that you have been using the power of your mind to produce the very limitation from which you wish to extricate yourself. Realizing that in your ignorance you may have been doing this, you need not condemn yourself or anyone else. Aware of the fact that you are a child of God, as we all are, you need to start to express your Divine heritage. As your thinking is patterned after your highest concept of spiritual Perfection, so will your life be a reflection of such thoughts.

SAY: Today, realizing that my life is truly a reflection of what I think, I now permit the Spirit within me to guide and direct my thoughts and emotions

The Divine influx refreshes me daily, and I feel myself saturated with the Life Essence Itself; I feel It flowing in and through me.

I now know myself to be a perfect instrument in Life's Divine Symphony, in tune with Its Harmony and Perfection.

My body is an instrument in, through and upon which Life plays a Divine and Perfect Harmony.

I do not search for other powers, for there is only One Power, the Power which I am going to use, the Power which I already know possesses eternity and is already at the center of my own life.

I know that this Power does now heal every condition, overcome every obstacle and free me from every false condition. And so it is.

Live Longer

For a long time there has been the idea that as we conserve our abilities and energies the longer we will live. Now it appears that in some respects this is all wrong. The particular thing we have reference to is brainwork, that activity most of us like to shun. It has been held for some time that intellectual activity shortens a person's life. Now just the contrary appears to be true.

A Swedish researcher has reported that those engaged in intellectual pursuits actually live longer than others. This is not the result of fewer demands on the physical body, but instead brainwork acts as a tonic and source of vitality for the whole body. In fact, other reports show that as far as the heart is concerned, it carries a comparable load whether we engage in mental or physical work.

One possible explanation rests in the fact that, in one way or another, almost every function and activity of the body is in some way influenced or controlled by what we think. If we allow ourselves to become mentally sluggish, the body follows suit. If we are continually disturbed and fearful, the body starts to malfunction. If, on the other hand, our thoughts are constructively active, it is logical that the body will similarly respond.

Regardless of how intellectually active we may appear to others, for ourselves we are mentally lazy unless we use all the mental ability we have and are continually seeking to further develop it. This is a personal equation which demands that we live up to the best we have in us. And the best we have in us is an unlimited resource we but little realize, let alone use. So start to think and live longer!

∞

Heritage

The kingdom of God is at hand. The riches, power, glory and might of this kingdom are yours today. You do not rob others by entering into the fullness of your kingdom of joy, your kingdom of abundance. But you must recognize that all people belong to the same kingdom. You merely claim for yourself what you want the Divine Spirit to do for everyone.

The eternal now is forever filled with the Presence of perfect Life. You always have been, and forever will remain, a complete and perfect expression of the eternal Mind, which is God, the living Spirit Almighty. You are a creation of Spirit and have Divine heritage.

SAY: Today I enter into the limitless variations of self-expression which the Divine Spirit projects into my experience.

Knowing that all experience is a play of Life upon Itself, the blossoming of Love into self-expression, the coming forth of Good into the joy of Its own being, I enter into the game of living with joyful anticipation, with enthusiasm.

Today I enter into my Divine inheritance, freeing my thought from the belief that undesirable external conditions imposed upon me are necessary and unchangeable.

I declare the freedom of my Divine sonship, and drink the fullness Life has to offer.

Mental Rabbits

We are always amused and amazed at the infinite variety and limitless number of things that a magician is able to pull out of a top hat. We may not be so good at pulling live rabbits out of a hat, but it is entirely possible that we are better magicians than we realize. In fact, the things that we seem to be able to pull out of our mental hat would make any magician look like an amateur, and there is nothing make-believe about what we do. It is all for real.

Let us see just how capable we are sometimes. We get in an argument with someone, one of those heated affairs which gets us considerably disturbed. We get tense and our heart starts pounding. Soon we find that our stomach is tied in a knot and the digestive process has almost ceased. By now we have no doubt forgotten the argument but we begin to worry about our stomach and the possibility of having ulcers.

We spend so much time thinking about this that we now develop a headache. Then aches and pains start developing in all kinds of places, which of course provide us with more props to put on an even bigger show. The big finale is reached when we have so exhausted ourselves that we can't go to work and no part of our body is functioning right.

It would appear that we need to become more aware of our unusual ability as a magician. Once we know what capabilities we have for causing ourselves trouble, perhaps we will be more careful as to how we use them. There is also the fact that this creative ability we have can be used for our benefit instead of our detriment. There are many wonderful things to be experienced in life. Let us learn to concentrate on pulling these out of the creative power of our thought.

∞

Invisible Good

You need to develop an understanding that although your body is real and tangible, with definite form and outline, it is at the same time somehow made of a living stuff which is saturated with God-Life. Whatever the stuff your body is made of, though it is called material, it must really be made of the Essence of which all things are made. Therefore, you need to sense within the very cells and tissues of your body an Eternality.

SAY: Realizing that the Spirit within me is God, being fully conscious of this Divine Presence as the sustaining Principle of my life, I open my thought to Its influx.

I open my consciousness to Its outpouring, carrying with It all the power of the Infinite.

I know that silently I am drawing into my experience today and every day an ever-increasing measure of vitality, health, joy and harmony.

Divinely guided, everything I think, say and do is quickened into right action, into productive action, into increased action.

My invisible perfect pattern already exists.

My faith, drawing upon this source, causes that which was unseen to become visible.

The harmonious action of Life now permeates every part of my being and experience.

All the good there is, is mine now.

The High Price of Living

For everything we get in this world there is a price that must be paid. Of course we all know that we keep getting less and less for the dollar we spend, but this is not the kind of price we are talking about. We pay for many things in a manner that cannot be measured in dollars and cents.

The outstanding medical researcher, Harold G. Wolff, M.D., after years of study summed up the idea very neatly when he said, "There are many things more important than comfort and even a few more important than health." Clinical evidence revealed the manner in which the physical body is ravaged by our patterns of thinking which are centered on strain, extreme emotions, anxiety, fear and other physically detrimental attitudes.

Take the case of a man who is making a very good living, but who is under such tension and strain in his work that he develops ulcers. He is confronted with the problem of changing his job and reducing his standard of living, or continuing on and being willing to sacrifice a degree of health for the increased income. Dr. Wolff says that "a man should appreciate what his actions and goals are costing him. Then if he chooses, he may pay for them in pain and disease."

Instead of sitting back and letting conditions, situations and problems overwhelm us, could we not develop an attitude of mind that lets us meet them and handle them in a manner that is intelligent and emotionally mature? When we learn to meet the problems of living without sacrificing our goals or comforts, we can have our cake and eat it too, and the price is controlled thinking.

∞

Physical Perfection

Your body is a temple of the living Spirit. It is spiritual substance. Since the Spirit of God has entered into your being, your life is spiritual. The supreme Being, ever present, exists at the very center of your thought. This Presence within you has the power to make all things new.

SAY: *I know that the perfect Life of God is in and through me, in every part of my being.*

As the sun dissolves the mist, so my acceptance of Life dissolves all pain and discord.

It remolds and re-creates my body after the likeness of the Divine pattern which exists in the Mind of God.

Even now the living Spirit is flowing through me. I open wide the doorway of my consciousness to Its influx.

I permit my physical body to receive the flow of Spirit in every action, function, cell and organ. I know that my whole being manifests the life, love, peace, harmony, strength and joy of the Spirit which indwells me, which is incarnated in me, which is my entire being.

I realize that all the Power and Presence there is clothes me in Its eternal embrace; that the Spirit forever imparts Its Life to me.

I know that the Spirit within me is my strength and power.

Getting Along with Ourselves

Most of us are familiar with the tantrums of children who are unable to have or do what they please. Sometimes they are quite a show and very violent. However, for the most part they are short-lived and the youngster goes on his or her merry way again. We feel that this is just a stage in the growing-up process and that the youngsters will get over it as they mature. But do they? Have any of us?

True, we may not put on an obvious show for others, but we may unconsciously do it for ourselves, keeping the body in a state of turmoil. When we are confronted with doing things that we don't want to do, or when we find ourselves having to do things at a different pace than we might like, medicine has found that the body often throws a tantrum in the form of a migraine headache, and in such cases tranquilizers have little or no effect.

If we can recognize the conditions and situations in our daily living which may contribute to a migraine headache or other conditions, then we can deal with them objectively instead of unconsciously reacting to them with a body tantrum.

However, unlike the child who gets over his or her problem in a hurry, we often are not fully aware of the nature of ours, and, as a result, keep ourselves in a state of turmoil for days, even weeks and months. Then instead of just having the outward problem, we also have an internal one which compounds the issue. The next time we find ourselves faced with a situation to which we might respond by saying, "That gives me a headache," we should try to change the reaction. There is more truth in our words than we realize.

∞

Self-Control

You are some part of the Divine Whole, and the Power and the Presence of the Spirit is in the word you speak, and that word instantly and perfectly and permanently makes whole. Know that you are an individualization of the Spirit— the Source of wholeness, love, reason and intelligence. Empty yourself of any and every thought that denies this. Know that, silently but effectively, the Divine Power of the invisible Spirit is working in you here and now.

SAY: I take hold of this realization with complete certainty.

I recognize that I am a perfect being, living under perfect conditions, knowing that Spirit alone is real.

I also know that Mind alone is the only thing that has any power either to act or to react.

Everything that I think, say or do today shall be thought, said or done from the spiritual viewpoint of God in everything.

My recognition of this Power is sufficient to neutralize every false experience, make the crooked straight and the rough places smooth.

Definitely I know that this recognition establishes harmony in my experience, prosperity, and a sense of happiness and health.

As I now discard and release all ideas to the contrary, I experience complete wholeness.

The Art of Getting Sick

Within us and all about us are those microorganisms which once given a chance merrily multiply, causing us untold misery and suffering. We live in a peaceful state of coexistence with the microscopic world until something upsets the applecart and some condition of ill-health seems to descend upon us from out of the blue.

There are many factors which could be responsible, but one that is receiving more and more attention is a person's job. Or perhaps it really should be put the other way around—not the job itself, but the individual's negative reaction to the job, which can become a highly developed art.

It appears that our mental and emotional responses to our work may cause such radical changes in our bodily functions that our defense mechanisms are lowered and we then find ourselves at the mercy of the microscopic world about us—in other words, we get sick. This is what so often happens to us but we don't realize why it has happened. Of course one solution would be not to work, but then we would no doubt find other ways and means to keep ourselves disturbed and upset with the same end result.

We cannot escape from living but this does not mean that we have to submit to and like everything that we encounter in our work or daily living. However, we can learn to develop a flexible good-natured approach to things we encounter and try to do something about them. We can make a good start in this direction by really trying to find at least one thing about our work that we can learn to like. This frame of mind can be contagious and before long we will have rebuilt our defenses.

∞

Love to Live

There is an eternal newness of Life. You are one with Life and the Spirit is continually creating in and through you. There is no darkness, despair or discouragement in the Mind that creates all. But people have sought out many devious ways to deprive themselves of the abundant Good that is always available to them. In your mind and thought is the key to successful living. You are the captain of your fate.

SAY: I have the will to be well, to be happy and to live in joy.

I affirm that there is only the likeness of good health in my experience.

I am seeing this good, believing in it, thinking about it and expecting it to continue.

All that I do I do with joy.

All whom I meet I embrace with thoughts of love.

Realizing that I am rooted in pure Spirit, I trace my life and being back to its original Source and know that every activity of my physical body is now in perfect rhythm with the One Perfect Life.

All my ideas to the contrary are discarded, eliminated. In their place there is established the complete conviction that my body is the temple of the living God.

I am made new and whole in this moment as the Love of God permeates me.

God's Life is my life now!

Learn to Kid Yourself

"Don't kid yourself." This we frequently tell others or are being told ourselves, the implication being that things are really not what we think they are. A lot of us do take particular delight in daydreaming and indulging in some sort of wishful thinking. Although we may not realize it, a great many people have developed this sort of thing to the point that it is actually a fine art and an extremely practical one at that.

Physically, mentally and emotionally we very often find ourselves down in the dumps. Everything around us appears to be wrong and we obligingly let ourselves follow suit. This indicates that we are letting our lives be dictated by things outside of us. Really it should be the other way around. We must deal with the experience of everyday living, but we should remember that we have a life of our own to live and should learn to direct it.

This is where we can start to learn to kid ourselves. When we find ourselves bogged down mentally, we start to think about some happy times we have had or anticipate having. If we feel at low ebb physically, we take a little time to think how wonderful it is to feel good, actually trying to mentally enjoy the feeling that we are in good shape. As for the emotions, when they are wrought up, if we force a smile or laugh we will soon be doing it naturally and tensions will be released.

If we consistently keep at it, we will soon discover we are actually experiencing the enjoyable patterns of thought we have systematically worked at creating. When we learn that constructive kidding is a very practical endeavor and a fine art, life will be more normally balanced.

∞

Receptivity

It is impossible for you to receive that which your mind refuses to accept. If you desire to receive more you need to consciously develop the ability to mentally encompass it. You make your life mean, little, and limit its possibilities when you refuse to accept the whole gift of God. As you open your consciousness to a greater receptivity of the Divine, to an enlarged concept of the good that can flood your experience, life will take on a new and wonderful meaning.

SAY: I now tell myself that my thoughts are filled only with a greater anticipation of a fuller life.

My thinking now expands and I know that a greater good than anything I have ever conceived is coming into my experience.

Without reservation I believe this and accept it as being so.

My mind and body are continually open to the Divine influx of all that makes for vital, joyous living.

The quiet but sure right action of God peacefully readjusts everything in my life as I surrender all ignorance, doubt and fear.

As I now cleanse my mind of thoughts contrary to my greater good, and come to dwell on only those ideas creative of health, wholeness and happiness, then does the abundance of God's kingdom fill every moment of all my days.

There is nothing in the Universe that limits you, or that would or could desire to limit you. There is nothing in the Universe that withholds from you because in so doing it would withhold from itself. You are some part of its purpose, therefore. The Spirit seeks, urges, pushes against you to fulfill itself. No matter how abundantly the Horn of Plenty may pour out its universal gifts, there must be a bowl of acceptance, a chalice of expectancy, or the gift cannot be complete.

—FROM *THE SCRAPBOOK* OF ERNEST HOLMES

IV

The Future Is Yours

The future is something everyone seems to dream of, but seldom does anything about. Tomorrow is always that wonderful time yet to be experienced.

You no doubt find yourself so involved in memories of the past and the immediate concerns of today that you more or less let the future take care of itself. The future always does take care of itself, but it is born out of what you are thinking today.

Your future is like a projection screen upon which are thrown the images of the thoughts you have today. It can be no better. It can be no worse. But at any time you can change that picture—change it to something definitely to your liking.

This does not mean you indulge in daydreaming, wishful thinking or idly hoping for the best. Your thought is a dynamic power, but for it to be specifically creative in your experience you must use it in a definite manner.

Limited Ideas

It appears that all too often we limit our thinking by the restricted meanings we give to certain words. This is pointed out by Harvard astronomer Harlow Shapley, who said in one of his books that all we know about the world we live in can be resolved into four basic concepts: space, time, matter and energy. But he asks the significant question: Given these four things, would it be possible to construct the universe? Or would a fifth factor be required? This fifth factor he refers to is a mystical entity which most people call God.

Dr. Shapley stresses the point that we should not "use up" this great concept by making it relate only to our individual lives and the particular part of the universe we live in. The nature of this master Entity which makes use of space, time, matter and energy to create in an intelligent way all things, animate and inanimate, we may never be able fully to understand. However, the fact remains that our concept of God should never be limited, for we limit ourselves to the extent we limit God. Just as we limit the nature of God according to our ability to think of God, so we seem to limit our health or success to what we consider "health" and "success" to be.

If there is one thing that appears to have absolutely no limitation it is our capacity to think; our thoughts are free to soar to any height. But too often we allow ourselves to think just so far and no farther. We make use of our ability to think to build barriers around ourselves which we are afraid to cross.

We need to let our thinking be a ladder to newfound freedom and a greater adventure in living.

∞

Expansion

Everything in the universe is a unique individualization or expression of the One Thing, which is the cause of all things. You should become aware that the one creative Power is expressing in you in a unique way and that It is always pressing against you, seeking a fuller outlet of Its infinite possibilities. You do not have to imitate or compete, for you are a special creation of God, as is everyone else, and you have full access to the unlimited potential of infinite Intelligence.

SAY: Today I practice being myself and seek to more fully reveal the miracle of Life. I discover a fuller delight in living and the wonder of Being that continually wells up within me.

I think simply and directly from the center of my being, which is God, the living Spirit.

I enter into the faith of believing, the joy of knowing and the act of living which proclaim the one Power and the one Presence in all things.

Today, as a child, I accept this Presence that responds to me as personal, warm and colorful. It fills me with vitality, opens my mind to greater vistas and imbues me with a love for all life.

As I now accept my partnership with the Infinite I discover a new freedom.

My thoughts soar, my experiences expand and unbounded joy fills my being.

What Counts

From all reports there continues to be an upswing of interest in things religious. From the lecturer's platform, from radio and television, floods of words on the subject are being poured out. Sometimes they make an impression on the listener, other times they only provide something for the listener to talk about. Is it not possible that all too often a person may have complete faith in the value of faith, have a belief in the effectiveness of sincere belief, without having either faith or belief?

Sincere faith and belief have amazingly salutary effects on an individual's health and in his or her experiences. But talking about faith and belief, and considering this as religious conviction, is a far cry from the actual thing. It is shallow, superficial and of little or no value. Just going through the motions of saying one is religious does not make one religious.

Basically, religion is an intensely personal thing. It is a way of thinking and believing that dominates every pattern of thought and is reflected in every act. It is not a part-time activity but a full-time endeavor. At its core, religion should contain an understanding of our relationship to our Maker, to our fellow humans and to the world about us. And its basis should be intellectually and emotionally sound.

To be religious is not as simple as donning a coat, indulging in conversation or participating in a socially acceptable activity. It is a way of life that touches and influences everything we do. What counts is not what we profess to be, but what we actually are. And what we are flows from what we consistently think, believe and have faith in.

∞

Individuality

Life has set the stamp of individuality on you. You are different from any other person who ever lived. You are an individualized center in the Consciousness of God. You are an individualized activity in the Action of God. You are you, and you are eternal. Therefore, do not wait for immortality. The resurrection of life is today. Begin to live today as though you are an immortal being and all thought of death, all fear of change, will slip from you. You will step out of the tomb of uncertainty into the light of eternal day.

SAY: I know that every apparent death is a resurrection; therefore, gladly I die to everything that is unlike the good of God.

Silently I pass from less to more, from isolation into inclusion, from separation into oneness.

Today, realizing that there is nothing in my past which can rise against me, nothing in my future which can menace the unfoldment of my experience, I know that life shall be an eternal adventure.

I revel in the contemplation of the immeasurable future, the path of eternal progress, the everlastingness of my own being, the ongoing of my soul, the daily renewed energy and action of that Divinity within me which has forever set the stamp of individualized Being on my mind.

Our Unique Ability

From the child making sand castles to an elderly man whittling a cane, from the exploring scientist to a person preparing a new dish for dinner, we find evidence of creative imagination at work. To be creative seems to be a fundamental drive that of necessity must find an outlet in a constructive manner if one is to be a full and complete human being.

It might be wise to take a good look at ourselves once in a while and discover to just what extent we are making use of this unusual asset.

To make use of our creative imagination does not mean that we necessarily become a great artist, composer, author, inventor or financial wizard. Rather it would seem that in all that we do, in everything we undertake, we must in some way discover how we may contribute something new and constructive to our world. We need to encourage the flow from us into all of our experience—more of that which is a unique expression of the creative ability of the mind within us.

Those who are able to do this are the ones who give the most to life; they are the ones who further the advancement of civilization; they are likewise the ones who create the happiest homes.

To enjoy a life that is productive of the greatest good for ourselves and others we need to express the most that we are. The most that we can be rests in our ability to think imaginatively and creatively. As we delve into the inner resources of our minds we will be surprised at the limitless potential that resides there. To think is to use Life's greatest gift to us. Why not start to use it more effectively?

∞

Perfect Activity

The all-intelligent, creative Presence is the source of all that you are. You need to believe in the ability and the willingness of this great Source to sustain Its own creation. The Kingdom and the Power and the Glory of God express through you. Recognize yourself to be a center through which the Intelligence and Power of the universe find expression. Infinite Mind, operating through you, can bring to you the manifestation of harmony, order and the highest good. Through It the consciousness of peace and plenty is established within you. All that is necessary to your happiness and well-being belongs in your experience.

SAY: There can be neither limitation nor lack in my life, for nothing has happened to the one perfect Activity.

As It now freely flows through me I am freed from any sense of bondage.

All power is given unto me from on High.

Knowing this, I am strong with the strength of the all-vitalizing Power of the universe.

I am sustained and inspired by a Divine stream of Spirit-Energy which flows through me as enthusiasm and vital ideas.

Every aspect of my mind responds to this spiritual flow.

Creativity and inspiration are my Divine birthright and I am now expressing them to the fullest.

A New Horizon

It is amazing how resistant our minds are to the influx of new ideas. All too often our thinking seems to be in a rut and we raise barriers which prohibit even casual consideration of anything we do not already know about.

An illustration of this is contained in a letter from a doctor connected with a hospital in Brazil. It seems that one day he was prowling through a used bookstore and bought a small bundle of American magazines which contained numerous articles on the effectiveness of affirmative prayer. He scoffed at the idea and even had some good laughs; tied the magazines up again and tossed them on a shelf.

Many months later he found himself confronted with numerous difficult situations in his life, problems which appeared insurmountable. In this desperate state he hesitantly turned to the magazines, dusted them off and started to read again. Completely skeptical, he nevertheless undertook to try the idea of creative prayer. He had nothing to lose, and no other direction in which to turn. He was amazed at the results. His words were: "It works! It works!"

There is probably nothing that we are less familiar with than the nature of the functioning and creative power of our own thought. Yet it is only in and through our own minds, that which makes us what we are, that we are ever able to accomplish anything. This creativeness may objectify in either a positive or negative experience, depending upon the content of the pattern of our thinking.

New and happier horizons of living will open up for us to the extent we learn to keep our thoughts directed in an affirmative manner.

∞

Resource

If you surrender your whole being to the Divine Spirit, knowing that of your own human self you can do nothing, you get rid of that self which is impotent. You brush aside its weakness, its fears, its doubts, its misunderstandings, and its uncertainties, and you think back to that Divine center within you which is God.

Come to believe in the power and presence of the Spirit within you. Accept Its power and permit Its guidance. Feel that you are speaking from this center of Divine certainty within you when you state: "There is One Life, that Life is God, that Life is my Life now."

SAY: I know that there is a Presence of Perfection at the center of my being.

I feel the Divine Life flowing through me, animating every atom of my being.

And I feel that everyone else is of like nature to myself—we all live and move and have our being in God.

I now affirm, with complete acceptance, that the Intelligence that created all things is now leading and guiding me into the accomplishment of every good and worthwhile purpose.

This Presence exists at the very center of my being and is flowing through me, establishing happiness, joy, abundance, harmonious living and a constructive use of the creative power of my mind. I am now open to new ideas, new hopes and new aspirations.

Modern Slavery

Disconcerting is a report which stated that one person in ten, in Western countries, is neurotic and in need of assistance. For years we have been spending all of our efforts in trying to build for ourselves a wonderful new world to live in. However, today things do not seem so bright. Instead of being masters of the situation, we now appear to have become enslaved by the society and culture we have created and discover that in many respects we are no longer able to keep pace with or meet the demands that it makes upon us.

The way things now stand we either have to learn how to cope with the problem, or else maybe nine out of ten will soon find themselves succumbing to the dire results of just trying to live in the world we have created for ourselves.

We seem to have two choices. We can either call a halt to the fantastic rapid growth of our culture, or we can discover a way to grow up so that we are once more masters of our lives, and do not just exist as automatons and slaves in a system from which we try to escape by retreating from life.

Collectively we can build our society, but individually we alone are responsible for how well we can grow mentally to cope with the pressures of daily living. This no one else can do for us. A fundamental starting point is a definite program for developing greater mental and emotional maturity. However, it must be realized that any maturity we may desire to attain can only be achieved by first seeking to grow up spiritually. This may not be an easy thing to do, but on it rests our chance of regaining our lost freedom.

∞

Joyous Living

You need to awake to a new joy of living. Whatever there may have been of fear, doubt or uncertainty in the past, realize that today is a new beginning. Your world can be made new from this moment.

Have the will to be well, to be happy and to live in joy. Recognize that there is nothing in your past that can deny you the privilege of living happily, and there is nothing in the future that can bring anything other than joy to you. Learn to find only the likeness of good in your daily experience. As you discover your daily good, and believe in it, and think about it, you expect it to continue.

SAY: Realizing that I am rooted in pure Spirit, I trace my life back to its original Source and find that every activity of my mind and body is in rhythm with the one perfect Life.

It is this Life that circulates through me now, eliminating anything that does not belong.

It now makes perfect every action of assimilation, circulation and elimination in my body.

Having the will to live in joy and in wholeness, I am at peace with the world about me.

It is my desire to live and to let live, to give and to forgive and to see in every person I meet the Divine likeness.

As I now release every sense of depression or limitation I am lifted up into a new joy of living by the Giver of all Life.

My heart sings a song of happiness and freedom.

Don't Be Contented

If there is one thing that most of us continually strive for it is to reach a state of contentment, where everything would be fine, our troubles and problems would all disappear, and life would become a blissful existence. Then we would have what we might call peace of mind.

But can we ever really reach a state of such contentment? Is peace of mind as desirable as we think it is? Although we like to feel we are making some progress toward attaining such a goal, what would we do when we got there?

Possibly the happiest person in the world might be the one who had just fulfilled a lifelong ambition and climbed the world's highest mountain. But then he or she would become a most sorrowful figure—no peace of mind, no contentment—for there would not be a higher mountain to climb.

Perhaps we have to revise our ideas about what contentment and peace of mind mean and provide ourselves with different definitions of them. They can only be considered as things to be actively experienced and not plateaus on which we just sit.

There is a Divine discontent within us. It keeps driving us on to greater goals, and it is the process of reaching these goals, not the goals themselves, which provides contentment and peace of mind.

Recognize this Divine discontent within you. It is the creative impulse which through the ages has urged people on to ever-greater achievement. Deny it and you deny your humanity.

∞

Peace of Mind

The Divine Presence is already what you are, and It contains the possibility of all joy in living. You should not entertain any thought that would limit your experience of the good life. There is nothing in you that can separate you from the Divine Presence, but in many ways you are able to inhibit Its flow through you. The greater possibility of knowing the Love of God, increased joy of living and greater good in your life is yours for the accepting.

SAY: I affirm that the Spirit within me is evermore leading me on the pathway of joyful living.

It is forever directing my thoughts, my words and my actions into constructive channels of self-expression.

It is forever uniting me with others in love, kindliness and consideration.

I live and move and have my being in the infinite sea of perfect Life, in the Divine Presence from which I cannot become separated.

I accept the Divine Presence as the great Reality.

I know that the kingdom of God is within me.

I have complete trust that the Law of Mind will make manifest in my experience my every good desire.

Everything necessary to my happiness is now established in Mind and does become an established fact.

Are You Responsible?

All of us seem to be burdened with an ever-increasing number of responsibilities. At times they seem so mountainous and so disliked that we go to any extreme to avoid them.

The odd thing is that very often more thought and effort are devoted to avoiding the responsibility than would be required in fulfilling it. The attempt to escape our responsibilities could cause more ailments and repercussions than meeting them.

It would appear that in our attempt to avoid outside responsibilities we are overlooking our great responsibility to ourselves—that of keeping ourselves in good health. In shirking our obligations we seem to be inviting physical complications.

We often attempt to escape from a situation through the use of tranquilizers. The sedation of a tranquilizer may alleviate our problems but it is not a cure. The cure rests in a mental discipline that permits a better adaptation to the life we are living—to develop a broader outlook, a more controlled pattern of thinking. We need to mature so we will be enabled to do what needs to be done and get over the attitude that we will only do what we like to do when we want to do it.

We will always have responsibilities of one kind or another, so it is not a case of getting rid of them, but rather of being able to fulfill them. A life without responsibilities would be a void. The greatest of all responsibilities is to ourselves—that of so expressing the Life within us that we fulfill Its need to expand and at the same time enable us to meet demands made upon us. It is then that we begin to grow up.

∞

Accomplishment

As you learn to release all your burdens to the right action of God, you will find that everything falls into its proper place. You let your problems slip away from you, realizing that a Power greater than you are, and a Presence that is within you, is ready, willing and able to guide you in all ways. Then peace, security and fulfillment come with ease and there is a sense of joy and accomplishment.

SAY: I now release all thoughts of fear, doubt and uncertainty, knowing that the infinite Intelligence of the Spirit within me knows what to do, how to do it and does it with ease.

This Intelligence guides my every thought and act.

Everything I do shall be a joy and shall prosper.

My every encounter with others shall be a blessing for all.

The right action that manifests in my life also works for all others.

Loving, I know that I am loved.

Giving, I know that Life shall give back to me.

Reaching back to that within me which is Divine, I now invite the Presence of God to make Itself known through me, bringing joy and happiness into my life and the lives of those about me.

Resting in calm faith and quiet expectancy, I know that there shall be only happiness and joy in every situation in which I find myself.

Educated Fun

There is an ever-increasing hue and cry for more pay for less time put in on the job. The added money enables us to have more of what we consider makes life easier and more enjoyable. But what about the additional time we have at our disposal? Probably a lot of it is used for indulging in sheer play and fun. We need to have a lot of complete relaxation for the benefit of both mind and body, but there is a limit to the amount of play that is good for us. Too much of anything leaves us with a feeling of oversaturation, and then what do we do?

We seem to possess a built-in sense of needing goals to be achieved, of having to experience a feeling of mental and emotional satisfaction for a worthwhile undertaking well done. This cannot be attained through purposeless play and time-killing amusement. Something more is needed.

We should conscientiously educate ourselves in the use of leisure time. The endeavor need not be overserious or labored time-consuming activity. It should and must be enjoyable, but at the same time provide us with an end result of being able to give forth the best we have within us.

Regardless of our age—be it twenty or eighty—the goal remains the same, but the sphere of activities would be different. And we should not overlook the fact that there is more fun in creating than in possessing. We need to educate ourselves in many ways so that we can squeeze out of our spare time the last full minute of constructive and creative achievement.

∞

Greater Possibilities

There is always the greater possibility available to you. There is a Divine Strength and an infinite Wisdom at the center of your being, ever waiting to be released, that will enable you to put more into life and living and to take more out of it. A limitless Creativity exists and expresses through all that is. It is always seeking a fuller channel of expression through you. Recognize that It exists, and accept Its action in your life.

SAY: I now lift up my whole thought to the inflow of Divine Strength and infinite Wisdom.

I know that I am in a silent partnership with God, today, tomorrow and every day.

I accept the creative action and direction of the Spirit within me.

I know that new doorways are opened, that new opportunities for self-expression are now presenting themselves.

New ideas are coming into my mind.

I am meeting new situations.

I expect to accomplish and achieve.

Divine Intelligence flows through me, inspiring me and directing me into ever more worthwhile goals of creative endeavor.

God guides me in every way and new horizons of joyous living continually open up before me.

I accept the fullness of Life at this moment.

Who's Confused?

When confusion arises we are always pretty sure that it is because of the other fellow, not us. Also, when relationships are strained it is always the other person who is at fault. And which parents do not think that their teenager is the most confused person on earth!

Investigation has brought out that the youngsters are not half as confusing as they are confused, and that many of their problems are compounded by their parents' own sense of anxiety and insecurity; parents find their own mental states reflected right back to them in the attitude and behavior of their offspring.

This same reaction can be found in any home, office or group of people. One person who is beset with worries and anxieties can contaminate the thinking of a whole group of people. When we find ourselves surrounded by unpleasant relationships, whether it be with our children, relatives or coworkers, perhaps before we complain about them too much it would be a good idea to carefully examine ourselves. The odds are that they are but reflecting back to us our own state of mind!

The only way to have our relationships be what we want them to be is to remember that what they are is but a reflection of what we are. If we want to experience good relationships we must first establish the idea of good relationships in our thinking, appearances to the contrary. This is the only way they can possibly be reflected back to us in actual experience.

In spite of how other people may *appear* to us they cannot be other than what they *are* to us unless we change our thinking about them.

∞

Harmony

You live in the house of God, as do all other people. The house of God is filled with people of Divine origin. They will become as Divine to you as you permit. As you look at them, they look at you, for this is the way of life. Everyone responds to you at the level of your recognition of them.

In the household of God there is no jealousy, no littleness or meanness. It is a household of joy, a place of happiness and contentment. There is warmth, color and beauty. Seen in this light your earthly experiences and associations are largely what you have made them rather than letting God manage things.

SAY: I know that in the house of experience in which I live the host is God and that all people are guests.

The invitation has been eternally written for all to enter and dwell therein as the guests of this eternal Host in joy, integrity and friendship.

I do now fully accept my Divine obligation to express only love and appreciation to and for everyone I encounter, knowing that only what I think, say and do can return to me.

I permit Divine Love to operate through me into my affairs.

Now only harmonious, happy and mutually beneficial relationships fill my life.

I rejoice in the Divine Harmony which surrounds me.

Cooperation

The famed founder of analytical psychology, Dr. Carl G. Jung, in an essay stated: "I am merely concerned with the fate of the individual human being—that infinitesimal unit on whom the world depends, and in whom, if we read the meaning of the Christian message aright, even God seeks his goal."

This very interesting observation seems to toss a considerable responsibility on our shoulders, one that we did not ask for, but one which might be considered as our reason for being here at all. When we come to think of it, the primary thing that separates us from all other living things is our ability to think. Are we using this unique ability to go on our own merry way, or using it in a manner that reflects the nature of the Power greater than we are which created it?

The Nobel Prize-winning physicist Robert A. Millikan said in his autobiography that the Architect of the universe has brought us this far and provided us with a mind and now it is up to us to use that mind. The intelligence and creativity that reside in the Universe flow through us and to the extent we cooperate with it we are cocreators in our world.

We probably never stopped to think about this before, but it is an idea of great importance to each one of us. We can cooperate with Life or combat It, aid or deter Its flow through us. If we cooperate with Life and express Its nature there is an influx of wisdom and an impulsion for right action.

How often do we cooperate? Seldom? Just sometimes? Or most of the time? It would seem that for practical purposes it is necessary that our thoughts and acts conform to the highest concept we have of the God that created us.

∞

Unity

You live because Life lives in you. You move because there is a universal Energy flowing through you. You think because there is an infinite Intelligence thinking through you. You exist because the Divine Spirit has sought to individualize Itself in and as you. This is why you are called the temple of the Living God. There *is* a Divine spark at the center of your being. But you need to recognize this, believe it and act upon your belief.

SAY: I now recognize my Divine birthright.

I consciously enter into my partnership with God in joy, love and a sense of peace.

I know that I live, move and have my being in the Life of the Spirit.

God seeks to express through me in a little different form than anyone else.

I now accept my responsibility to be what I truly am, and to live up to all that Life seeks to be through me.

There is a place in my mind that merges with the Mind of God and I now draw power and inspiration from it.

The radiance of the Presence of God envelops me.

In this knowledge of Unity with God, everything in my life is constructive, life-giving, blessed and prospered.

I joyously express the Nature of God.

INDEX

ABOUT THE AUTHOR

Ernest Holmes (1887-1960) was the founder of the Science of Mind philosophy and movement. Ernest Holmes's teachings are based on both Eastern and Western traditions, and the empirical laws of science and metaphysics. Science of Mind is a spiritual philosophy that people throughout the world have come to know as a positive, supportive approach to life. These ancient truths have kept pace with and proven their relevancy in today's global village and its expanding technology and warp-speed changes.

Author of *The Science of Mind*, the seminal book on his teachings, Holmes also founded the monthly periodical, *Science of Mind* magazine, which has been in continuous monthly publication since 1927.

Through lectures, radio, television programs, tape recordings, books and magazines, Ernest Holmes has introduced millions of people to the simple principles of successful living that he called "the Science of Mind." His other works include *Creative Mind, This Thing Called You, How to Change Your Life, Words That Heal Today, La Ciencia de la Mente, Effective Prayer* and *This Thing Called Life.*

Also from Ernest Holmes

How to Change Your Life

"The wisdom of God is within you, and you can use it to improve your life."

How to Change Your Life presents:

- Ideas on life and God essential to contemporary spiritual understanding

- The merging of science and spirituality—what this means to you

- How to use Science of Mind to improve your experience of life

Code #6862 • $10.95

If you're ready to positively jumpstart your life, this is the book that can help you do it. Change your life by changing your thinking.

Words That Heal Today

"We need not lose our personal sense of being but should discover it in a universal unity from which good alone can flow. We shall find that our intellectual and emotional capacities become deepened and sharpened through conscious communion with the Spirit."

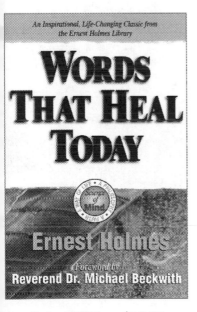

A treasured favorite among motivational and inspirational books, *Words That Heal Today* focuses on the teachings of Jesus of Nazareth and the Apostle Paul. It will show you how to understand the keys to the effectiveness of these teachings and how to apply them to contemporary life in all its dimensions.

Code #6854 • $10.95

Can We Talk to God?

This inspiring classic offers you a framework for prayer that is compatible with traditional religion, yet moves beyond it in the recognition of a divine presence within each one of us.

- What is the nature of God?
- What is our relationship to God?
- How do we communicate with God?
- What is the secret of spiritual power?
- Where is humanity headed?
- How can a prayer be used to help ourselves and others?

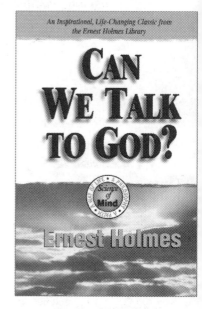

Code #7362 • $10.95